CW00840383

The Wash

just some more poems

Andrew MacLaren-Scott

Copyright © 2018 Andrew MacLaren-Scott

All rights reserved.

ISBN-10: 1727183134

ISBN-13: 978-1727183139

Andrew MacLaren-Scott

The Wash

It will all come out in the wash, they say
in the great, grand wash of Time
with the spin cycle of our good Earth each day
and the soak and the suck of the tide
And every disruptive distraction
will disperse to much less than it seems
as everything currently consuming us
dissolves like yesterday's dreams

Okay as me

The sun on my face
the gentlest of breeze
a glass of refreshment
my fine lady to squeeze
The wash of the water
the wisps of high cloud
a good planet turning
a hill high and proud
The green and the gold
the sun bright and warm
the strangest of feelings
that it was good to be born
A purpose that beckons
A reason to be
A quiet realization
that I'm okay as me

As I was

Everything ruined by worry
was I
Every fear that existed
was me
Every disaster was waiting
to fall
Every demon my number
to call
Every day was a struggle
to live
Every night was a trouble
to dream
Every dawn an unwelcome
awakening
Every birth a reminder
of death
Every smile a grimace
a sneer
But...
nothing to fear, to fear, to fear

but fear

I hear

The cynical appraisal

Corruption is rife

and petty small fiddles

the bribes and backhanders

and commonplace diddles

the cash in the hand

and the nod and the wink

the preference of buddies

and the done deals that stink

the seedy deceits

in the snatched secret meets

the men and the women

with their quick cheating screwing

the hands in the till

and the rigging of votes

the stitched up agendas

fixed with sly secret notes

To cheat is to live

to live is to lie

it's the way of the human

from start until die

Spiralling through

An end is always a beginning
a beginning is always an end
though not of a circle
but a spiral
with time as the twister that bends
and spins and pulls and changes
and thank goodness for that spiralling too
as a spiral offers much more of interest
than circling a circle could do

Perthshire walking

In the gentle rolling hills of Perthshire
In hidden green clefts and among high trees
I still sense the young men slowly walking
Bearing arms and off to war
My dad among them, fresh and eager
To the haunting call of wild wood pigeons
Walking, gathering, walking on…
Then back they came
But only some
Heads now filled with sounds of gun
And by Blair and Burrelton, Guildtown, Clunie,
I still sense them all in the Perthshire sun

Ignorance

We don't know what anything is, really,

fundamentally

And we don't know why anything exists, really,

fundamentally

Our descriptions always end in mystery, eventually

Our explanations always end in mystery, eventually

We can use, modify and manipulate,

wonderfully

But we don't know what, or why, anything is,

fundamentally

Romantic really

Don't love me, no
Just like will do
Don't ask for love
but I'll like you too
Don't let's pretend
it's always happy end
But let's keep it going
while always knowing
we are not all good
but still not bad
One lovely lass
One lucky lad

In Memory

Labelled difficult by those who could not get you to
do what they wanted you to do
or to say what they wanted you to say

Labelled left by those expressing views to the so-
called right of yours and labelled right by those with
views to the so-called left

Put in a labelled box on the basis of one specific view
while taking views that were such a complex mix
from all across the range

Called negative when you tried to introduce some
sense of reality into some ambitious dream

Called unrealistic when your thoughts threatened to
disrupt another's comfortable scheme

Told you believed there is no god when all you had
said was that you did not believe there is a god while
confronted by those unable see the vast distinction

You have upset, and have been upset

You have been unfair, unpleasant, foolish, and… oh,
foolish, and foolish some more too, but sometimes
wise, give you your due

Sometimes kind, true

You confessed your sins, but not to any priest

I heard

You messed things up, then messed some more when
trying not to mess again

I saw

You tried to love, but failed

Have been loved, perhaps, perhaps not, but lost

Lived, and for too long, you sometimes said

And now, it's done, you've died, you're dead

Now, you are… well no, you are not even dead

Just nothing now

Nothing, nothing, nothing, but a memory in my head

And I strive to remember every detail of that sole and final thing you said

The words, the groan, the grimace, gasp and clasp

Your most important message was your last

Aileen's song

Your universe is vast and wide
but part of hidden greatness
beside you and inside of you
of spaces you can't access

That is where the secrets lie
of how you come to be here
the pointed process and the why
so far from you, but near

The masters and the servants
the creatures and their minds
offer only fleeting glimpses
of the truths you cannot find

Now

Now is almost nothing
but is all that does exist
Gone before you grasp it
but the only thing there is

The problems

One of the problems with growing older is that you have to live with the consequences of a steadily increasing number of poor choices and mistakes.

One of the problems of growing older is that you learn more each day about how stupid people, including yourself, can be.

One of the problems of growing older is that you can see the problems of growing older more clearly than the benefits, of which there are a few.

One of the problems of growing older is that it never stops, until it stops, and it rarely stops nice and cleanly, as we can all observe.

One of the problems of growing older is that it does eventually stop, and it becomes increasingly apparent that it may stop soon.

One of the problems of growing older is that growing older can turn you into a miserable old git with a tendency to dwell on all of the problems of growing older.

And one of the problems of growing older, is growing older.

But, as they say, tomorrow is another day, perhaps for gloom and glum to blow away.

That's that then

That's that then
today is all that matters today
forget tomorrow until today is away
a road behind
a road ahead
and me in the middle
still alive in my head
some things done
some more to come
still here on a rock
circling a sun

I sit therefore I wonder

I frequently feel that I just need time to sit and think

But when I get time to just sit and think

My mind wanders and I fidget

Wondering what it was that my sitting and thinking

was meant to let me do

So I sit and I think: "what was it that I wanted to sit

and think about?"

Until the moment passes

And I move around doing things

While thinking:

"If only I just had time to sit and think"

Decisions

Chemicals can't decide

Can't take decisions

Unless there is much more to chemistry than we

know

So brains can't decide

Unless there is much more to brain biochemistry than

we know

Biomolecules bounce around and react by physical

and chemical law

Sustaining our thinking somehow

But how?

We can't decide

No really, we literally can't

Unless there is much more to us than we know

What is a thought?

What is a thought?

We don't know

A specific pattern of nerve cell activity, perhaps?

But we don't know how or why

a pattern of nerve cell activity could create a thought

And what is a memory?

We don't know

A recorded and repeated pattern of nerve cell activity, perhaps?

But we don't know

What is a mind?

A self?

A conscious living, loving, hating, thinking, remembering being?

We don't know

Always remember

Always at the start of something
While in the Bubble of Now
Always avoid looking back
Or worrying about what may come
Always just accept the situation inherited
And plan to build and move on
Stop the negative thinking
Remember it's the attitude that matters
The thinking can make anything different
Live the day, in its best way
Come on, come on, come on.

The Human Beings

Idiots

Who claim to know things they cannot possibly know

Who follow, mimic, copy, lie

Pretend, bluff, bullshit, connive,

Cheat, steal, deceive, conspire

Mess with nature and play with fire

Geniuses

With powers to understand what seems impossible

And achieve their miracles of mind and molecule

Build, grow, share, revive

Heal, help, transform, survive

Idiots

Who claim to know things they cannot possibly know

Who follow, mimic, copy, lie

Pretend, bluff, bullshit, connive,

Cheat, steal, deceive, conspire

Mess with nature and play with fire

Things that messed me up

Some things that messed my mind, and life, are

Reading - so called worthy literature that made me

gloomy

Learning - things that made the nature of life so clear

Thinking - too much, too deep, too hard

Beware of reading, learning and thinking

They can mess you up

Just living is better than thinking about living

sometimes

The hardest words

The three hardest words

it seems

are "we don't know"

although we don't know

what matter really is

why anything exists

how life began

how consciousness arises

or what it even is

so what we, as conscious minds, actually are

and if there is or are a god or any gods somewhere

among so many other things

that we just don't know

but find it so very hard

to simply, humbly, sensibly, say so

Without doubt

Stop doubting yourself

But forever keep doubting yourself

In order to achieve

the improvements

that will justify stopping doubting yourself

Have confidence reinforced by doubt

Does that make sense?

I doubt it

Another day (please go away)

Another day

another person interfering and trying to manipulate

what I do

Another day

another person talking nonsense and expecting me to

agree

Another day

another person being ignorant and rude, oh no, it was

two

Another day

another person trying to change me from the

perfectly acceptable way I want to be

Another day

another mindless idiot spouting faith in things they

cannot possibly know are true

Another day

another unwelcome and unasked for interruption to

the business of being me

Another day

Just leave me damn alone, the lot of you, please do,

please do, please do

Andrew MacLaren-Scott

The unbuilt boat

There is a man building a boat
and it begins to seem clear that the boat will never
float
no water will ever wet its bow
except the rain that halts the construction
again, again, again
which does not matter
may even help
for in the building of the boat he finds a purpose
even though the boat will never be built
and were it to be built he would realise
that it could not sail
perhaps not even float
so it is important that the man should never stop
building his boat
but should never finish
building his boat
for it is the building of the boat
that keeps the man afloat

30

just building, building, building

the boat

that will never float

It is time

It is time

Just look at the clock

It is, isn't it?

Come on now

You know what for

Or perhaps for what

even if I do not

and I certainly know what for

Or perhaps for what

even if you do not

It is time

It really is

this time

Think about it

and you will know what it is time for

or for what it is time

And like me you will have thought about it a lot

but the knowing is not the problem

It is time to move on from the knowing

and get started on the doing

It is time

this time

It is time

to do, not talk

Just look at the clock

ticky-tock

ticky-tock

tick-tock

Coexistence

Coexistence is possible

if you leave me alone

and I leave you alone

and you don't try to change me

and I don't try to change you

We may never be friends

but we may coexist

Demented

Another one seems to be going now, so sadly,
although he is 93
His real being disintegrating each day before us, is
dreadful to see
A grey shadow, turning black, creeping over a once
bright mind
A stumbling, emerging, confused, incoherence, as
consciousness turns blind
Light ebbing from a darkening evening sea
And so who next?
Maybe her, him, you, me

Don't dare smile

One little girl who smiled at me
was enough to cheer me up
until her mother saw, and snapped
although in a whisper, but one I heard:
"Don't smile like that at strangers"
and looked at me as if I was so bad
to have smiled so freely back
Well fair enough, in this dreadful place
to warn and keep your small child safe
but sad, still sad
And when the same child looked back at me
and half-smiled again, in a somewhat conspiratorial
way
I turned my head to pretend not to see
I am so sad to say

Angry

I can get angry

And this day I was so damn angry

I was walking in the street shouting

"Ahhhhhhhhhhhh! I'm so damn angry!"

Until the glare of a woman with a child I had not

noticed shut me up

I mean I had not noticed the woman or the child

not just the child

I was so damn angry

At what?

I'll tell you what…

Oh… let's skip softening lies and jump to true

I am angry at you, yes you

and me

At people

oh, and pain

and cold and wind and rain…

At life and death and mud and mess and guts and

gore and more…

At planets stars - the whole damn lot

of Universe's messed and muddled ugly plot

Unwinding right behind my eyes

beyond the woman, child, the dark grey skies

Ahhgngry!

Happy not...

. . . .

But settling now?

Maybe...

Yes?

Or maybe not

We get the world we make

dumped out in a blackened void?

Alone

Forgot?

This festering fetid human lot

(I feel better now)

The Colleges of King's and Darwin

In grand King's College Chapel
mighty stones are raised so high
An astonishment of roof work
in masons' manufactured sky
Stained glass tells famous fictions
And some travellers sit and pray
washing the pain of living
in God's care, they may well say
But back by Darwin island
sitting on carpentry wood
I take in Nature's cathedral
the trees, the grass, the good
Here I find my own salvation
in the truth of Nature's way
Contemplation of the mystery
is the only way I pray

Good words

They don't just come when commanded,

they have to be born by themselves,

but when they come good they come easy,

as if created by somebody else.

The flow is dictated by rhythm,

the thought is dictated by mind,

and once here they are often discarded,

awaiting for someone to find.

The Grim Healer

The Grim Reaper is The Grim Healer

He cuts your trouble from sight

with one *swipe* of his clean sharp scythe

And everything that ever mattered

and bothered

and troubled

tormented

and tortured you

will be gone...

with one *swipe* of his clean sharp scythe

And the sweet Healer *will* come

so do set today's troubles aside

'till the job of his healing is done

with one *swipe* of his clean sharp scythe

Oh.............................

with one *swipe* of his clean sharp scythe!

That's that then

Three years younger than me…

slim, healthy, but dead…

Walking around on Monday,

working, discussing what lay ahead.

Now cold on a slab today, Tuesday,

people reciting the last things he said.

"Next week, tomorrow, the meeting…

the deadline, the problem, the strife.

Cheerio then, we'll discuss that tomorrow…"

Hours later, departed this life...

The need to be free

I need to believe in freewill

at least as a possibility

for the sake of my sanity

and so I need to believe in things we don't know

that leave us room to decide

for what we know of the physical world at present

leaves no room for a free mind to choose

without things we don't know about

being added, but what are those?

Don't Care

I've done all the sad

now I'm going to try happy

cos just feeling bad

is obviously crappy

This may not be profound

nor even fine rhyme

but it beats being gloomy

every damn time

There is light in my head

Did a pill put it there?

Well frankly my friend

I really don't care

Nobody knows

Nobody knows what anything is really

Matter, atoms, particles, bits...

It all collapses into words

described by numbers

equations

changing

describing what nobody knows actually is

really

And the things I see out there

are really in my head in here

back there in a bit of brain

with my forehead far out there really

beyond that farthest mountain

that I see in the model

created in the deep dark bits of my brain

and refreshed, again, again

but just a view of what nobody knows really is

really

out there

in there

everywhere

These days

Few people do anything useful

these days

making or doing things

that are actually required

Few people understand

how to make the technology we rely on

or how it works

Most people are pretty much incapable

of anything useful

these days

But they are useful

to a degree

because they can watch TV

and buy things

and create demand

for other generally useless people

to do useless things to meet

while they moan and bleat

and live, and eat

Untitled

Is this a poem
or is it prose?
It rhymes a bit,
but also stutters, somewhat, as it goes
Just words together
that is all
thought walking when the clocks go back
and the dark nights begin
and I, for one, say 'bring them in'
for I like the seasons
as one of the reasons
for walking out, then walking in
And I have realised I often find it easier to be
cheerful
when some people expect things to be bad
easier to defiantly find happiness
when some expect me to be sad
I do like the spring, but somewhat fear the summer
for when sunshine shines I sometimes, obstinately,

feel glummer

I'm smiling now, indeed I am

so you smile too please

if smile you can.

Switch in mind

Mental switches:
little thoughts
that change a mind
Start from now
just accept what got
remember the young lad
with a life to find
Starting over
Starting over
from now
from now
from nowhere else
Abandoning worry
to leave a mind empty
awaiting the future
just living for self
for self is plenty

Just

We live in a world of changing season
with effects that must each have a cause
but within that may lie deeper reason
or things that are just there because
Not beginning or ending or affecting
just always and always and on

So is everything just here for ever
in a world that is endlessly stuck
in a cycle of repeated repeating
which is possibly just our tough luck?

And it's never the thought that's the problem
The problem is in the belief
There's nothing silly in wondering
but's it's silly to think that we know
if knowing just cannot be justified
as most claims of knowing cannot
It may not be easy not knowing

but that may just be the problem we've got

Fatty McDonalds

Fat family in McDonalds
including big Fatty Jim
sitting around messy wrappings
and feeding his son who is slim
The boy is only four
and he'll be feeding and feeding much more
'til his belly is fat and eyes dim
In Fatty McDonalds
he'll be stuffing his face
with burger and chips and fat cheese
and breeding and feeding
and feeding and breeding
more fat please
more fat please
more please

More is lore

We do not know what matter is

Electrons are enigmatic

Molecules are sculpted clouds of electron-negativity

surrounding hazy points of positive charge

Things are moving and interacting

pushed and pulled

by electromagnetism and gravity and more

And the energy of everything is dispersing

But venturing any deeper is just dreaming... lore...

To be

I have endured the most ridiculous nonsense

The most challenging despair

and yet here I am

still here, or there.

So what now?

Most certainly not self-blame and guilt

but moving forward afresh, as me,

as simply what I want to be

Now (and then)

One thousand years

a century

a day

a moment

now...

a million

billion

trillion

endless time

and then again

somehow

Beethoven, Bach, Rachmaninoff

the vibrating atom

the molecules in the head of dullard and Prof

and then, and now

again

and how

the fields vibrate

the energy disperses

the universe sings

its endless verses

one thousand years

a century

a day

a moment

now...

a million

billion

trillion

endless time

and then again

'til now

somehow

The best of the worst

The worst ignorance

is to be ignorant of our ignorance

The worst certainty

is the certainty there is no uncertainty

The worst thoughts

are the thoughtless thoughts

The worst words

are the words that hurt

The worst hurts

are the hurts by words

and the worst response

is to despair

The worst days

are the days of failure

but the best days

are when failure triggers

the best response

which is to build

and to repair

and looking back

to say

that the best day

was that worst day

there

the worst day

the best day

the best

is there

is here

Clear?

Go

And thus it begins

all over again

but always different

What?

We'll see

Maybe

Let's go

No?

Neither do I

What?

Know

Ocean in

The ancient ocean lives
in every cell
and in the rich red river blood
the clever chemical interaction
the ebb and flow of life in flood

What is there to say?

What is there to say

That has not been said?

Apart for new discoveries

Is originality dead?

What could we say

In any case?

Just let me think…

We know a lot

But not enough

The mysteries are so deep

The reason for anything

The fabric of matter

The origin of the mind

And the degree of freedom for that latter

But listing unknowns does not take us far

to being original about the way things are

Friends?

Friends affecting me

with vague shadows of relationship

inviting me to conform

while I resist

to be accused of oddity

contrariness

stupidity

all wrong

as friendship is going

going

gone

Fast lane

My friend is dying

but he told me,

"So are you,

Your illness is life

and it is fatal."

And I said, "Yeah but…"

but he interrupted me with,

"Yeah but yours is worse eh?"

"Worse?"

"Yeah, yours is slow, and tedious, probably,

but me, I'm in the fast lane,

until sometime this year, most likely."

And he smiled

And I smiled.

It was good to smile

with a friend who is dying,

faster than me (probably).

The resilience of a child

I need to rediscover the resilience of a child

Look at how they cope

Brush off

Move on

Adapt

Survive

And live alive in the days and the weeks

So strange, that those fragile can be so strong

And I do need to rediscover the strength and

resilience of a child

I block the light

I block the light

stand in the way

I irritate and annoy

I interrupt, I misconstrue, misrepresent, delay

I criticize, and condescend

belittle, and I lie.

I fabricate, embellish, exaggerate and blame

I damage and betray and hurt

I'm useless at this game

I try, and fail, and try

and fail, and then I try again

Tomorrow, come tomorrow, with today's mistakes all
done

I'll waken to a fresh new dawn, then make errors one
by one.

I block the light

I hide the sun

I just get in the way. That is what the bad thoughts
say

until the bad thoughts go away

The man died

The man died this month

He was 86

I was sad, in a way, but accepting

But those relatives who are religious

are still distraught

And yet at his funeral they spoke of him being with

God

Indeed they spoke of him still existing

Yet they are distraught

even though they apparently believe they will have

eternity with him again

I don't understand why they are distraught

when I am the one who thinks he is gone, forever

and they just think he is in "a better place"

and to be met again soon

So why are they distraught?

I just don't understand

Rebuilding

The secrets lie in attitudes
and not in the events
the greatest being to start anew
with what the past presents
Awake, return, review, move on
Do something better than regret
Rebuild repair, improve, progress
Look forward and forget

We don't know

I picked up a book on consciousness
So many words
That could have been replaced with
"We don't know"
I turned to a book on freewill
So many words
That could have been replaced with
"We don't know"
I looked at the big philosophy text
So many words
That could have been replaced with
"We don't know"
And then the holy books
All side by side
And still we just don't know

Watching bats

Bats are darting erratically
as bats tend to do
The planet is turning
as planets do too
The only point in it all
that I can elucidate
is to live your life and try to appreciate
whatever you build will soon decay
enjoy the moments and live the day

Ennui

Is that it?

he asked himself

on being take on a special trip by his mother

to find just a grassy hillside

and boredom setting in soon

Is that it?

he asked himself

when she promised a special cake

and he found it to be just sponge and cream

Is that it?

he asked himself

when first stealing a young girl's kiss

and finding just an awkward rubbing together of skin

Is that it?

he asked himself

on about the twentieth time with a woman

as initial enjoyment began to seem routine

Is that it?

he asked himself

in the second week of each new employment

as new became old

Is that it?

he asked himself

as the doctor described the cancer

then brought the encounter to a close

Is that it?

he asked himself

as the nurses wheeled his bed to the side room

awkwardly commenting on the sunshine outside

Is that it?

he asked himself

lying alone

and waiting for his deep disappointment to be done

Water under the bridge

Standing by the bridge
that goes across the river
watching all the water
flowing slowly by
thinking of the time
of other water but same river
standing there before now
struggling not to cry
but now that river water
is the only wetness near me
flowing past the bridge
beneath a heavy sky
and I am standing by the bridge
that goes across the river
feeling life still passing
flowing on until I die

The Fires

The fires do burn themselves out
The fires of anxiety, worry, despair
The fires of passion, interest, and doubt
The good fires and bad
The happy and sad
The moments of frantic, that clench a tight hand
The moments of the desperate, need to understand
The intrigues and puzzles, the dramas and angst
All fires that burn across the mind's flickering land
Their end is a blessing when troubles burn fast
The feature of fires is they're not going to last

Printed in Great Britain
by Amazon

20067308R00047